MEATLOAF

MARRIAGE

What Do They Have In *COMMON?*

A simple, yet profound book with

over 40 years of marital experience

reminding couples why they married in

'the first plate.'

"I mean in the first place!"

By Peggy B. Dixon

MEATLOAF
&
MARRIAGE

PEGGY B. DIXON

Meatloaf and Marriage

Peggy B. Dixon

Copyright 2017 by Peggy B. Dixon

Cover by Brandon Bradley

ISBN: 978-0991554140

Bel Ekri Publishing

Acknowledgements

I thank God the Father for giving me the ability to express through words which help unify marriages. I thank God the Son for loving me enough to sacrifice his life for mine that I might have eternal life and for allowing me opportunity to fulfill the plans God has for my life. I thank God the Holy Spirit for educating me and for comforting me through the marriage journey.

Sister friends: Denise Guillian, Barbara Meeks, Anita Winbush, and many others thank you for encouraging me to stay on course and for keeping me accountable. I honor you all individually and collectively.

To my cousin Therese Dialls and sister friend Dr. Deborah French Keys, I humbly thank you for editing my book and your enthusiasm which made this experience invaluable.

My sincere thanks to Brandon E. Bradley for believing in my vision for marriages and for a breathtaking design cover.

To my sister Intercessor Vickie Powell for laboring over this book with prayer, I am much obliged.

Bless you Joy Harris for hearing and obeying the voice of the Lord. I appreciate you for helping me to bring my dream of writing *"Meatloaf and Marriage"* to a reality.

Dedication

Walter R Dixon, I thankfully dedicate this book to you. I have an amazing and wonderful marriage because of you. You are an awesome and exceptional husband. You're an incredible man of God. You're a remarkable 'Father' and role model. Thank you for praying for me and encouraging me to fulfill God's plan for my life. And thank you for loving me unconditionally. I love you!

I dedicate this book to my children: Reesa, Cyrus (Stephanie), and Rachel Dixon, and God daughter Yashica Kearse. I am so grateful to have you in my life. You are God's reward and my gift to the world.

To my remarkable grandsons: Darnell, Joel, twins Walter & Wesley, God granddaughter Myasia, to all my nieces, nephews and future generations I happily dedicate this book to you. Marriage is so worth it.

Forward

Meatloaf and Marriage is a simple, but profound book. Anyone that is married or has been married can relate. Meatloaf and Marriage is a great book to have as a tool for those about to marry. Meatloaf and Marriage is an ideal book to have especially for those in their first year of marriage. And Meatloaf and Marriage is a wonderful book to refer to after you have been married for a while.

Intercessor Vickie L. Powell

Foreword for Meatloaf and Marriage

For as long as I've known her, Peggy Dixon has had a deep love for the Lord and a genuine call to teach, to exhort and to write. Ministry can take many forms. When we first met, we were both young wives and mothers. That was our ministry. For Peggy, the form it took during those early years was in training her children and especially in loving her husband. As her sister-friend I got to witness the way she kept the sizzle in her marriage with special little effort and creative touches. I really appreciated the way she safeguarded their privacy while sharing enough for me to tweak her ideas for my own marriage. And by the way, she did all this without making her marriage seem perfect or like her husband walked on water. I never got the impression that they didn't argue or have hard times. But I did see a spirited-filled wife who took the time to figure out ways to be a wife as well as a mother. I wasn't the only one who benefitted from her practical wisdom. By word and example, she showed new and seasoned wives how to stay connected to and interested in their husbands. Without being fully aware of it, Peggy was in training to be the Titus 2:4, woman who could teach her generation, as well as future wives to love their husbands. Meatloaf and Marriage has been a long time coming. It is the response to request to "please, write this down!"

I am family life educator. I have spent my professional life working with couples and have a good idea how marriage get off track. More often than not, marriages erode, not explode. Erosion happens when couples allow little foxes to spoil the vine. Little foxes? Distractions, irritations, neglect, and nursed grudges are all little foxes. They may seem to be pretty annoyances, but when ignored they have the potential to wear away the affection and lightheartedness that gives marriage so much pleasure. When Peggy told me she wanted to write a book about marriage I knew it would provide down-to-earth solutions to everyday 'little' problems.

You're going to enjoy this book. From the first page it is engaging, funny, and thought provoking. The thing I like best about Meatloaf and Marriage is that Peggy focuses on what works. The message of this book is deceptively simple. Deceptive because, at first glance, the message looks easy. However, the high number of divorces testifies to the fact that though the message may be simple to understand, it is anything but east to carry out. The beauty of Meatloaf and Marriage is that Peggy has mastered the art of using examples, stories and questions to permit us a peek into the marriage she has nurtured for over 40 years. Meatloaf and Marriage is like having a warm conversation with a trusted friend who skillfully offers advice without being preachy, and then gives us a little something to ponder. Get ready for an excellent book that is a stealth weapon in the God's arsenal to bless couples and make you a little hungry for meatloaf!

Deborah French Keys, Ph.D., CFLE

Table of Contents

INTRODUCTION

The title of this book is to catch your attention and draw you in. And now that I have you thumbing through the pages, I'm sure you have noticed each sub-title starts with a question.

I ask questions because questions need answers. I ask questions because questions provide information. Sometimes questions are asked because the person asking the question needs or wants information from you. Other times the questions are asked of you to get you to thinking. So you are probably asking yourself, "What do Meatloaf and Marriage have in common?" And the answer is found in the pages of this book.

Two questions often asked somewhere in the world are:

1. "Will You Marry Me?"

2. "Do You Take This Person to Be Your Wedded...?"

Most of the time the response is a *'celebratory yes.'*

The questions in this book are designed with just that in mind to get you thinking. Thinking about your own marriage. The questions are designed to show you what you can do to help hold your marriage together while enjoying it as well.

I believe some questions in this book will have you smiling. I believe other questions in this book will put a puzzled look on your face as you read them. However, all the questions in the book are intended to help you become a better spouse. So enjoy the book as you would my meatloaf, if you were eating some. And if you want seconds, in my next book you'll get the meat of marriage.

1

COMMITMENT

When making a meatloaf mixing the ingredients together is only part of the process. Just like hearing the person officiating the wedding it is only part of the process the married couple will experience. It's the commitment to put all the right ingredients together.

You said, "I Do", But to "What?"

You glowed like a candle reflected in a mirror warm and inviting, while his ceaseless smiles set upon you like stars twinkling in the sky. So it was no surprise when everyone received your wedding invitation. After all the two of you had been dating for years. The running joke among friends and family was when you see one you see the other because you were always together. People called you the couple of the year before you were ever married to each other, and you were.

You looked absolutely radiant and your spouse looked magnificent on your wedding day. You loved being married. It was exciting. It was fun. He made you laugh and you made him happy. You held hands in public. You sat as close to each other as you possibly could without being on each other's laps except for in private. You ate out often and took lots of mini vacations. You enjoyed each other's company and you didn't want anyone intruding on your time together.

But after a while, the two of you started drifting apart. You didn't have the same interest anymore. You no longer enjoyed laughing together about anything and one morning you ask yourself as you look in the mirror, "Do I really want to be married." It had started. You started questioning the marriage. You looked at your wedding picture hanging on the wall, "What will become of the couple of the year now?" You're frustrated about the whole thing and you want to talk to someone about your situation, but who? Can you talk to your parents, his parents, your pastor, counselor, co-worker or your best friend? You decided not to involve anyone. You don't really won't them in your business or taking sides with your spouse. And of course your spouse would feel they would side with you. So you keep all your feelings to yourself and you bottle them up inside.

During the courtship you saw the differences that were between the two of you, but, you thought to yourself it will be ok. I can live with it. You think he'll change because you know you really don't need to change and he thinks you'll change because he doesn't think he needs to change.

Neither of you anticipated that being married to the love of your life would cause you to doubt whether or not you had made the right choice to get married. You were certain when you exchanged your wedding vows that this person was the person you loved and wanted to spend your life with. You never expected to have to make so many adjustments in the marriage. You never thought you would question yourself.

Yet on this specific day however, you think to yourself, "What have I gotten myself into?" You think, "I know I said, I Do, but, I had no idea it was going to be this bad or this hard."

You didn't imagine marriage would be so exhausting or challenging especially, after experiencing such a wonderful honeymoon and how amazing the first year had been. What had gone wrong? What was going wrong? Why did my mate change?

The answer is he hadn't changed and neither had you. The truth is reality had set in. You found out he doesn't pick up after himself, leaving things everywhere. Clothes stacked like mountains on the floor. He found out you fold everything neatly and put them away like you are organizing a clothing drive. There's a sink full of dishes while the dishwasher is empty and just a few steps away. Trash cans need trash bags. Towels are on the floor when there's two towel racks just above them. His snoring keeps you awake and he says you talk entirely too much. You complain he watches TV or plays video games all the time. He complains you never want to cook anymore. You both complain the other person left the gas tank on empty.

"What did we get ourselves into?" You say to yourself. The bills keep coming like reams of notebook paper while the cost of living rises like skyscrapers, and you haven't had any children yet. Only one of you believes in budgeting. Neither one of you can seem to get on the same page.

He wants sex and you want rest. You want help with the laundry, dishes and housework and he wants his needs met. You understand him to say one thing, and he understands you to say something else. You make the bed before leaving for work. Your spouse says, "Why fuss over it, we are just going to mess it up later." And the list continues on.

The covenant agreement has gone sour. You beg and you plead please help me out. You try being patient. You hope for some accountability on their part. Finally, when enough has become more than enough, you ask yourself, "What have I done?" "Did I make a mistake?"

These few questions racing around inwardly began to manifest themselves outwardly as your emotions are now on display like a thermostat. One of you promises to change; yeah right! But you can't because you have some deep seated things rooted down inside you that have to be plucked up. You can't not until the thing which is masquerading itself inside you has been exposed. You can't not until the thing that brought you to this place of, "I don't care anymore," has been removed or not until the thing that's causing you to want to give up has been uncovered. You can't not until the thing causing the tension between the two of you is dealt with. And more importantly you won't change until you make a concentrated effort to commit yourself to your spouse and the vows spoken at your wedding.

One is to commit to themselves to their marriage regardless how difficult or challenging things can be.

And there only a few exceptions. Your commitment in the marriage allows you to become the solution for breaking down walls and removing the barriers that keeps you from having a successful marriage. Being committed in your marriage is something you have to decide to do regardless how demanding the marriage can be. Being committed in a marriage is what you do because you made the choice to say, "I DO."

SO YOU'RE INVITED TO YOUR
OWN PRIVATE CELEBRATION
And here's how it works!
It's For: You and Your Spouse
Date: Whatever date the two of you decide.
Time: Whatever time the two of you decide.
Place: Anywhere the two of you choose.
Attire: Something romantic.
The Occasion: 'I Vow to Vow Ceremony,'
To breathe life back into your marriage.
RSVP: Private Ceremony, No Other Guest Allowed.
Sponsored by: You and Your Spouse

Because this time when you say, "I Do" You Will Already Know What You Are Getting Yourself Into!

What's For Dinner?

The greeter opens the door, greets you with a smile and tells you how lovely you look. You're wearing a black sleeveless beaded dress. Your spouse is wearing a black double breasted suit and tie, who is parking the car.

"Good Evening and welcome to our establishment." Your respond, "Thank You," and smile back. "How many are in your party?" asks the hostess. You reply, "Two," As soon as your husband makes his way through the door the hostess announces, "Your table is ready," and you are escorted to your table. Upon being seated she announces it's been a pleasure to serve you thus far, and then makes the statement that your server will be with you momentarily.

You were impressed with the hostess/greeter and equally impressed that she never used the word waiter, but server. You personally prefer the word server over the word waiter. You have found that waiters don't always make you feel special while in their establishment. Nor do you feel that they will assist you the way you would like to be assisted. Many times you feel disconnected. To have a server who understands serving is a blessing.

The restaurant atmosphere is cozy, with an air of elegance. Your table is draped in fine black linen with white linen napkins, there are three forks, two spoons, a knife for cutting meat, a butter knife, two water goblets, glasses for tea and cups turned down on saucers for coffee. The table reveals no salt and pepper shakers. The table doesn't reveal any sugar or sugar substituted packages. These things are concealed hidden away in a little black box sitting on the table. The menus' are located in a black leather book. The table is fabulous. But the highlight of your table are the fresh cut red roses.

Your server, though not dressed in shirt, tie or suit, certainly looks professional with his chef logo collared shirt and his black tux pants. The server announces I am _____ and I will be your sever tonight. He offers drink suggestions for the evening and then asks, "What drink can I bring you tonight? Would you like that with or without ice." When he returns with your drinks he ask to take your order. After several questions concerning the menu, you place an order. You were extremely pleased at how patient your server was while you were deciding what to order.

Throughout the evening, your server stopped at your table to make sure everything was ok. "Did you find everything to your liking?" "May I get you anything else?" He even offered some dessert suggestions without being pushy. Of course, you make a joke about your weight and order one despite the added calories. Everyone laughs because you know he hears that all the time. You remark to your spouse, "He's been a good waiter – no a great server, he served us with excellence."

So the question is how well do you serve your spouse? Sometimes when my husband is watching TV, I fix him a plate of food, when asked. Sometimes I'll get him a bottle of water or a glass of juice, when asked. He enjoys it. But what he really enjoys is when I serve him something without being asked. Especially, his favorite sherbet. He's thankful not just for the sherbet, because I thought enough of him to serve him without his asking me to. This I do graciously. This I do willingly. This I do with a smile.

But let me be honest with you there are times when serving him feels like a dreaded chore or maybe serving him feels like he is imposing on my time. Maybe it's not a dreaded chore or that he is imposing on my time. Maybe it's my approach or attitude about serving him and what serving him is all about that needs tending to and needs adjusting. Perhaps I need to correct the way I view serving. Perhaps I need to correct the way I view serving my spouse. Is it possible I need to look at the way I am serving my spouse?

One might serve you great food but with the wrong attitude. Yet the right attitude might determine the amount one's tip might be. You see you don't mine tipping your server more than you had anticipated when they have served you well. So here are a couple of marital tips.

Tip #1. We should be kind to one another

Tip #2. We should serve each other in love

Tip #3 We should be excited to serve each other

And a final tip is, "You commit yourself to that which you serve and you serve that which you commit yourself to."

The title of this chapter ask the question, "What's for Dinner?" Yet, the real question ought to be, "How's Your Serving?" Let me bring this to your attention, it's not only what you serve that counts, it's how you serve it.

Perhaps, if you and I serve cups of love, plates of kindness, and bowls of consideration to our spouses our spouses would show more gratitude. Maybe they would show us how much they love us, then respecting one another wouldn't be such a challenge for us. The thing that separate waiters from servers is one's willingness to serve.

"Are you committed to serving?"

"Are You Willing?"

What's Your Secret Ingredient?

My husband raves about my meatloaf and when my two older grandsons come over for dinner, the first thing they ask is, "Did you make a meatloaf?" Or they ask, "Are we having meatloaf?" Sometimes the answer is yes, to which they celebrate with thundering sounds "yes" and "I can't wait for dinner."

If my response is no, they groan in disappointment as if they are going to starve. But my older grandsons are not the only ones that love my meatloaf, the four year old twins love my meatloaf also. When they want more they say, "Mooorre pleash!" Other family members and friends request my meatloaf as well. This is because they say, "My meatloaf just melts in their mouths."

So I'm often asked if I have made one lately or am I planning on making one in the near future and they really mean the near future. They could have just had meatloaf the week before but to them it doesn't matter because they believe I should make one every week.

As I am writing this I can hear one of my sister friends saying, "Girl, I don't know what you do to your meatloaves. But girl you show know how to make a great meatloaf." And then I hear her saying, "What's your secret ingredient?" Then we laugh.

We laugh because we know cooks don't reveal their secrets. We laugh because we understand that even if we were to use the same ingredients, it wouldn't come out the same as mine. We laugh because we know that although each of us would have a good meatloaf, the appearance, texture and the taste would still be different. We laugh because we know mine would still taste better. It's not that I am a better cook than her, she's a phenomenal cook. It's that we each understand where our specialty lies and mine is meatloaf.

And so it is with marriage. You have got to include the right ingredients to make it hold together. You have to be committed to working at your marriage until you have perfected it. You have to understand that just like when you are cooking your favorite dish you may use a secret ingredient, in your marriage you have to have a secret ingredient as well.

When I cook a meatloaf, I use hamburger, onions, green pepper, Mrs. Dash seasonings, as many eggs as needed to hold it together, slices of bread or cornbread, ritz crackers, one minute oatmeal (raw). You may be saying, "I use those ingredients as well."

Then I add my secret ingredient. Something so simple. Something that should go into every recipe and it's the same ingredient that every marriage needs as well. It's the one ingredient that holds the marriage together during the toughest times. It's the one ingredient that can help make any marriage better. LOVE! Imagine that love is the secret ingredient that holds your marriage together during the

rocky times. Imagine that love is the one ingredient that brings a balance to your marriage when your marriage is going up and down like a seesaw. Imagine love is the one ingredient that only you can add to the marriage to help make it better. And imagine that over time, being committed to loving your spouse, just because he or she is your spouse can help determine the success of the marriage.

Now don't get me wrong, not every meatloaf I have made has always turned out right. Sometimes it didn't turn out right because the meat turned out to be bad meat. Sometimes I didn't add enough ingredient of one thing or the other. Sometimes I overcooked it or undercooked it. And there have been a few times I have burned them. Yet, the one thing understood by family members and friends regardless how my meatloaves turned out they know each one was made with love.

So whether it's a recipe for making a meatloaf or a recipe for making your marriage better add the one ingredient that will never fail. Add the one ingredient that is fail proof. Add the only ingredient that only you can add. Add 'LOVE!' All the 'LOVE' you want to it. Then watch how your family, your friends and your spouse rave about your results.

Did You See that Tackle?

Football is my husband's favorite sport and I will occasionally watch a game or two with him during football season unless he is watching a really close game. I otherwise consider myself to be is a 'bowl gamer.' I like watching championship games. It's something about all the excitement that goes into these games. It's something about the crowd and the multitudes that gather for the game. It' something about watching the enthusiasts. It's something about watching all the fanatics and it's something about seeing who will come away with the trophy.

When I went to junior high and high school football games I would watch the game a little. I really was there to socialize more than anything. So my responsibility before leaving the game was to get the score before I went home. I needed to be able to tell mom if we won or not and what the score was. This was mom's way of checking to make sure I had attended the game. Not to mention, she would already knew if I had attended the game anyway.

She had her spies, so she was always able to verify my attendance. You get the point.

What I like about watching football is which team recovers the ball after it has been fumbled. I enjoy seeing how far a player can run the ball before getting tackled. I will, however, admit I love watching the players make touchdowns, especially when a pretty pass had been made. I can just envision it now.

I bet because this paragraph started with the words, what I like about watching football is, you have probably detected that there's something I don't like about football.

You are so right. So, let me share my least favorite part of the game. TACKLING. It makes me cringe. I'm thinking about all those bodies being piled upon that one player. I guess I'm concerned about all the weight that the one football player is experiencing. I'm thinking about the possibility of a player getting injured.

But before you decide to tackle me with all your comments, before you start trying to explain the play book to me, I understand that being tackled or tackling another person is part of the game. It's football. I get that. However, I just don't like the tackling part except when my favorite team is losing. Have I just contradicted myself? I apologize.

I do understand you can't win a game without each person on the team being committed to the game even though they might get tackled in the process. I realize you can't get touchdowns without effort from every player on the team. This is the way it is with team sports it's the understanding that you have to work together for a common goal even if there are a few injuries along the way.

Sometimes a player is able to run the ball from one end zone to the other. Other times a player can only go so many yards. And not one person can single-handedly tackle every person on the opposite team and run the ball at the same time. There are times the ball gets fumbled. And still other times the ball is intercepted by the opposing team. So for either team to win the game it takes being committed to the game and to the players on your team.

However, while watching football with my husband, I have come to understand that there is one thing that marriage and football have in common. It takes a committed team effort to make it work. In football there are players on the opposing team that will try to hinder a player from making a touchdown. Yet the player doesn't give up and stop trying to reach his goal and neither do his teammates.

This is the way it should be with married couples. When you are faced with life's obstacles you work together to correct the problems. When one plan doesn't work you try another. You ask each other for suggestions. When things seem to be falling apart in your relationship, like a ball being fumbled, you run fast to catch hold of it. When things start piling upon you, you don't just sit on the sideline without being part of the solution. Get in there and help lift the load that is weighing your relationship down. Tackle those things together that are trying to keep you from having a successful marriage.

And when you are penalized for making wrong choices, with good sportsmanship, humble yourself and take it. It's one of the ways you can find out what your weaknesses are and another way in which you can help to strengthen your marriage. When you don't reach your goal keep trying. Don't give up. Don't stop trying. When your spouse doesn't reach his or her goal, forgive them. Make a plan, run with the plan and if needed get come coaching. Most teams have about three or four coaches.

Just as each player on a football team has different responsibilities the team works together to reach their goal.

Now, here's a 'PLAY' never to be forgotten. Although, you have different responsibilities in the relationship you should work together to reach your goal not only for you and your spouse, but for those sitting on the sideline and those watching in the bleachers trying to decide if marriage is worth it.

2

COMMUNICATION

To produce a successful meatloaf you need to season it correctly. In order to produce a successful marriage, communication is the correct seasoning.

Is There Static on the Line?

Have you ever tried to explain something to someone, but they weren't listening? What was your response? What was your reaction? Where you frustrated or just determined to be heard? Did you give up? Did you elevate your voice? Was the thing you were trying to say more important than you listening to the other person? Maybe, they were listening, but just wanted you to stop long enough for them to be heard. After all, it's the number one break down in marriages, the lack of communication.

To complicate things, now cell phones, tablets, laptops, and desktop computers are forms of communication. We text, blog, tweet, e-mail, Skype, and FaceBook and use all types of technology and social medias to achieve communication with one another.

When I was younger, telephones were our source of communicating with someone down the street, around the corner or across town. These types of phone are obsolete now except for those used for décor. It had a heavy base which usually set on an end table or a small telephone table. This table was much like sitting at a school desk. To use this particular phone you would pick up the held handle which we called the arm of the phone. The handle had a small round piece with holes in them at each end. The top part of the arm was for hearing the person talking to you. The bottom part of the arm was for talking to the other person. The handle and the base were connected by a spiral cord. After you picked up the handle, you would then put your finger in the slot which corresponded to the number you needed and dialed that number to make your phone call. We now push buttons, numbers or we use voice activations to accomplish the same thing.

When I was younger the closest thing to electronic toys we got were "Walkie-Talkies."

The first walkie-talkie I remember receiving was attached by a string. The second walkie-talkie I had was operated by batteries. Both toys I received at different Christmas'. They were great toys which allowed one to use one's imagination. While you were glad to have the string walkie-talkies, you were limited by them. These walkie-talkies only stretched about a yard or so apart from each other. Because the walkie-talkies could only stretch so far, you and the person at the other end had to agree which direction you were going to move. You couldn't go left while the other person went right and you couldn't go right when the other person was going left because the string only went so far. If you both went too far in the opposite direction, you would end up pulling the string apart.

However, having the battery operated walkie-talkie meant you weren't as limited. You could be in separate rooms and still hear each other as long as those rooms were in close proximity to each other.

The walkie-talkies allowed you to pretend you were a police officer. You could pretend you were talking to another police officer. Having the walkie-talkies helped to keep you informed were the bad guys were. They allowed you to pretend you were a spy. They allowed you to pretend you were spying on your parents and your siblings. You were excited to have walkie-talkies because you could hide behind furniture, you could hide behind doors and whisper and you didn't have to worry about the enemy hearing you. And when you got tired of playing the role of the good guy, having the walkie-talkies helped you be a bad guy running away from the police.

Were there problems with having battery operated walkie-talkies? Yes, there were many problems. If the walkie-talkies were too close, static occurred. Extremely loud static on the line often ended when someone yelled, "You're way too close!" "Back off some!" Sometimes you dropped the walkie-talkie because the static hurt your ears. Oftentimes the static kept you from hearing one another and you tried elevating your voice over the sound of the static which defeated the goal of having the walkie-talkies. Static on the line caused division. The static disrupted the environment around you and caused the enemy to know where you were hiding.

Learning to operate them effectively required patience. Only one person could speak at a time, otherwise you wouldn't be understood by the other. Sometimes you would be having so much fun and suddenly the walkie-talkies would stop working. You would punch buttons over and over hoping that would help them to start working again. But they didn't. You knew then that you had dead batteries and that they would have to be replaced. You would look around the house for more batteries only to find out that the ones you found weren't the right size. You took batteries from other things that also used batteries, like portable radios. At times this didn't work either because the charge in those batteries was low also. It was at this moment you knew for sure play time had come to a halt or at least playing with the walkie-talkies was over until you could convince your parent or parents to buy more batteries. Who knew when that would be? So for now you had to communicate with each other the old fashion way talking with each other without any devices.

Marital communication is much like using walkie-talkies. Someone talks, the other person listens or that's the way it should be. Sometimes one mate will try to out talk the other mate. And very often someone in the relationship is so determined to be heard and not necessarily understood that they scream, holler or yell at the other. Sometimes one of the person's in the relationship walks away to give each other cool down time before continuing their conversation. Sometimes one of the person's in the relationship walks away to keep from saying something they would regret later. Sometimes someone in the relationship will just shut down and not say anything. Then suddenly explode down the road.

One cannot assume that just because a conversation has taken place that communication has also taken place. Communication is a language. It is the language of being heard and being understood by the other person whether it's your spouse or someone else. Though you can use many different forms of technology when communicating with someone, perhaps face to face is still the most effective, because you get to hear what they are saying as well as what is not being said. You also get to see their body language.

Communication is best achieved when both people stay calm. Communication is best received when you allow the other person the opportunity of being heard over your own voice being heard. Communication is best received when you can trust the other person. Communication is best received when you are honest with one another. Communication is best received when you have respect for one another. And more importantly communication is best attained when the two of you talk.

So I suggest if there is static on your marriage line ask yourself, "What is it that is causing the static in the relationship?" Then ask yourself the following question, "Are you being selfish?" Ask yourself, "Is your opinion the only opinion that matters?" Ask yourself, "Does it matter who gets the credit?" Then ask yourself, "What, would you do if your mate were no longer at the other end of the line to talk to you?"

Don't forget walkie-talkies are only effective when the people using them work together to keep the static off the line. Remember, walkie-talkies are only effective when they are fully charged and when they are turned on. Could it be that effective communication is a turn on?

Can't You See That...?

What a person sees when they look at an ink blot depends on their perception, which may be due to their own personality not the influences around them. One person may see one thing while the other person sees something different. Sometimes both people see the same things, but at varying degrees. It just depends on how each person approaches the things they are looking at. Many times we only see what we want to see. And that is true when it comes to marriage.

You talk with your spouse about a certain issue or situation and you express your opinion hoping that your spouse will agree with you. But you find out your spouse doesn't hold the same viewpoint as you. It's understandable because men and women approach things differently. Men are logical and they reason things out. Women are emotional beings and make decisions out of their emotions. For example, when men build houses they see structure and framework. Women see rooms with furniture and painted walls. So here in lies the reason there are breakdowns in communication.

THE APPROACH

It's no one's fault that men and women look at things differently. However, what is our fault, is that we don't try to communicate those differences. It starts with not respecting the individuality of your spouse and thinking your spouse shouldn't have their own opinion about things. Then the blame game starts. The wife blames the husband and the husband blames the wife. Your spouse is not you, and you are not your spouse.

You don't think like your spouse and your spouse doesn't think like you. And for this you should be grateful. I'm sure that if you both approached everything the same way all the time your relationships would be boring. Your marriage would be humdrum. We need our spouses to think or view things differently. That's how you work to develop strong marriages. It's how you build longevity in marriages. It's realizing you both contribute valuable opinions to the relationship.

Looking at life's ink blots can provide you and your mate with a point of reference for conversations. Let me ask you what are life's ink blots that you and your spouse view differently?

- Finances: Spending or Saving!
- Children/Grandchildren: Spoil or Not to Spoil!
- Parents: Yours or Mine for the Holidays!
- Work or Career! Day or Night Shift!
- Purchases: New Car or New Homes!
- Church: Yours or Mine!

Ink blots are designed so a person can look at them and determine what they see or what they think they see. Maybe, if we take the time to discuss life's ink blots with our spouses we can see things from their point of view, and we won't always be asking, " Can't you see that?"

You Want Me To Do What?

Is it communication if you and your spouse argue with each other? Is it communication if you and your spouse scream, shout or yell at each other? Some would say, "No." Others would say, "Yes." The truth is it is communication. Negative communication. The kind of communication that is often demonstrated because of one's own frustration.

So how do arguments materialize? Sometimes arguments take place when one person in the relationship feels a sense of hopelessness. Sometimes they occur when one spouse is disappointed with the other. Sometimes they spring forth because of misfortunes, calamities and setbacks the marriages is experiencing. Many times though, arguments are voiced out of fear. The of failure. And almost all arguments occr of selfishness.

We often see arguments as
off our chest but without co.

anguish it might cause the other person. We see them as a form of speaking what's on one's mind without necessarily counting the cost for the behavior.

I am not saying that you or your spouse won't have disagreements. All couples do for one reason or another. But the truth is, two intelligent people ought to be able to sit down and carry on a conversation without screaming or hollering at each other. Shouldn't two wise adults be able to communicate with one another without yelling at each other? Shouldn't two intelligent adults be able to speak to each other using appropriate language rather than degrading each other with inappropriate language? And shouldn't two loving adults be able to talk to each other without throwing things at each other?

I'm not saying couples won't raise their voices to each other from time to time. What I am saying is that being heard and understood by the other person and expressing one's self without making a ne is positive communication.

At the time of this writing my husband and I have now been married for forty plus years. I remember in the fourth year of our marriage my husband and I had an ARGUMENT. I got so upset at him I threw a white ceramic lamp at him. The lamp hit the wall and shattered into tiny little pieces. I was grateful it had missed him.

I was really mad. Mad because he made me mad enough to throw something at him. Mad because we no longer had a lamp to use anymore. Mad because I had to clean up the broken glass by myself. Mad because the broken pieces had shattered all over the room. Mad because it was getting dark outside, and I needed as much light as possible to see all the shattered pieces that needed to be picked up. I was really upset. Upset because my husband left the house.

Because of pride, I wouldn't humble myself and apologize. So I told him, "Well if you don't like it you can just leave." He did just that slamming the door behind. I'm upset we had argued. I was upset that I had lost the argument. I was furious. I was furious because I hadn't gotten my way. After all, arguments usually occur because someone feels they are being overlooked, ignored or disregarded. I was mad because I was mad. In fact, I wasn't just mad, I was angry. Really angry. What sense did that make?

It didn't take long before I realized that this behavior hadn't accomplished anything. It didn't take long before I realized I didn't have any justification for being mad, upset, furious or angry. It was my own action which caused a re-action. After all I loved my husband and really didn't want him to leave me.

So when he returned home although, I was still not over everything that had happened, I did apologize for starting the argument. I apologized to him for breaking the lamp. Oh, did I mention the lamp was a wedding gift from my husband's mother? So my throwing the wedding gift my mother-in-law had given us showed just how immature I was at that time. It showed how much I needed to grow up. It showed how selfish I was.

We had several more intense conversations after that day, but I never threw anything again. I admit, I wanted to, but I didn't. I purposed to talk things out with him sensibly. I finally came to realize something, if we were going to survive as a couple, we would have to do things differently, NO! I should I say I learned I was going to have to do things differently.

Well over the years I have learned some conversation lessons I would like to pass on to you.

First, I've learned arguments never accomplish the thing you want them to.

Second, I've learned it's not only what you say, but how you say it.

Third, I've learned he and I could truly disagree without being disagreeable.

Fourth, I've learned that if I say it in love, I could say whatever I wanted to say and he was at least willing to listen.

Fifth, I've learned you don't have to have the last word.

Six, I've learned that my body language speaks just as much as my mouth does.

Seventh and the most important lesson I've learned is you don't always have to say anything.

Maybe that's the difference between negative communication and positive communication. Knowing when to speak and when not to speak. I think that's called love in action, rather than reaction.

3

GUARDING YOUR MARRIAGE

The containers (though not an ingredient) you cook your meatloaf in helps to determine the shape of the meatloaf. So it is with marriage, guarding your marriage helps to shape your relationship.

Who Moved Now?

When you see a checker board set up you might assume someone is about to play the game of checkers. You might assume the same thing if you see a chess game set up. Both games require you to think about your opponent's next move as well as your own before making a move. Thinking through the process helps and may give you the opportunity to have the edge over your opponent.

When you see a moving truck sitting in someone's driveway it usually gets your attention and you assume that someone is moving out of the neighborhood. But that doesn't always have to be the case, sometimes someone is moving into the neighborhood. However, what is evident is that someone has made a move.

When it's a Friday afternoon and you are caught in traffic you are wondering what side street, road or highway you can take to avoid the non-moving traffic.

As a parent, when a small child is right up under you and you are trying to get things done, what you want from them is to go and play. Yes, play and play anywhere but not right up under you. How about the times when you are trying to put the clothes in the drier and they pull them out faster than you can put them in? And what about the times when they are screaming or hollering about wanting something to eat or drink, but they refuse to move out of the way so you can get to the necessary things that will fill their hunger or thirst. All you want them to do is move. Unwrap your legs and move. Finally, when you have had enough you let out a "MOVE," but of course they don't. They want what they want and they want it right then and there.

We have talked about chest and checkerboard players making their moves. We have talked about people moving in or out of the neighborhood. We have talked about traffic not moving and about small children who won't move from right up under your legs.

Now let's talk about the time when my husband and I went to visit a friend in Phoenix, Arizona. We were in flight and I fell asleep. But, when I woke up, I asked the question, "Are we still moving?" To this my husband replied, "Peggy of course we are still moving. We are 1000's of feet in the air." To which I replied, "We are not moving." And just about the time my husband was about to say something else to me the pilot came on the intercom and said, "Ladies and Gentlemen we have been in a holding pattern for some time and we are going to have to land in Tulsa. And that settled that. We weren't moving.

Now, let me ask you have you moved?

If you are a woman I can assure you that we have moved away from our spouse at one time or another. Remember when you used to sit right up under him in the car. But as time went on and the routine of being together day in and day out wore off, you moved from sitting right up under him. Especially if you were having intense fellowship.

Hold on, the men aren't off the hook. Our husbands move from us too, because at some point in the relationship they stopped asking us to go on dates with them. They still loved us or still love us. However, they just generally don't do the date thing much after you marry. The wife is generally the one who asks, "What do you want to do?" Or we generally ask how about going this place or that place. We are the ones who say, "How about if we do this?" You get the idea.

It was the dating that allowed the relationship to grow stronger to the point you knew you wanted them as a mate and they knew that wanted you. You got to know each other's likes and dislikes. You discussed your past, present and future together. You talked about places you would like visit. You talked about whether or not you wanted children and how many.

But you didn't talk about what you would do if you two found yourselves not moving in the same direction. Not to worry, I have a few suggestions. I strongly suggest you just start dating again on a regular basis. Once a week and for sure once a month. Ok, I hear you saying, "What with my job, with church, my business, with school, the children, cooking, cleaning, laundry, and grocery shopping and more even with my spouse's help? How can I?

Remember, a proposal was the first thing done when the man knew he had found his good thing.

When he found the one he wanted to spend his life with. The one he was sure he wanted to marry. Well I have a proposal for you and your spouse. Whatever date you got married on you should at least attempt to make that your date night. For example if you got married on the tenth, then on the tenth of every month that would become your date night. Arrange It. Schedule it. Make plans although the plans may have to change. Yes, go ahead and put it on the calendar because there's something about scheduling it that helps to make it possible. It makes it conceivable. Making these little adjustments helps ground your relationship and your commitment to each other.

Dating helps to guard and protect your marriage from the many things that distract in a marriage. Dating helps to keep communication lines open and helps to energize the intimacy of your marriage.

After all, the day and date you got married was the day you started moving forward together and it became the most memorable, 'DATE' of your lives.

Should it ever stop? The fact is your proposal was a onetime event and the marriage is forever or at least it was your thinking when you said, "I Do." So go ahead make those reservations. 'Cause if you don't make them, time still moves on regardless

Are You Standing Guard?

There are various ways to protect oneself or one's interest. When you ride a bike or you are skateboarding it is advisable that one should wear a helmet and elbow and knee pads to protect oneself. When you drive a car you wear a seat belt for protection. You put your car in park to keep it from moving so you and others don't get hurt. You put locks on windows and doors because you want to keep your possessions safe. There are police to protect our communities. There are laws to protect our land. There are banks to protect your money. There is even toothpaste to protect the enamel on one's teeth. There's nail polish to protect your nails, and lip gloss to protect your lips.

When I grew up, my family and I would watch westerns on Saturdays. We watched: "Rawhide," "Rifleman," "Roy Rogers," "Gun Smoke" and one of my favorites "Wagon Train." It was something about the way families traveled in covered wagons from one part of the country to another part of the country not all being kin. It was something about the way all the campers looked after each other. It was something about them living in covered wagons with barely enough room for their family or supplies. It was something about them sitting around the campfire talking and dancing. Sometimes they held a dance around a campfire to give the people something to do and to help elevate the thought of danger to the campsite. Yet, you knew when they held a dance around the campfire and the music changed in the background something exciting or adventurous was about to take place.

One phrase I remember spoken in particular was, "Whose standing guard tonight?" The trail guide or guides were concerned about cattle rustlers and horse thieves. The guides were concerned about being able to pass through Indian (Native American) territory. They were concerned about protecting their personal belongs. Keeping their supplies secured doing the journey was essential to their survival. It was their responsibility to make sure the cattle got to the cattle drive on time. Doing so meant the difference between making a little money or making the amount of money you contracted for. And they were especially concerned about their family members getting across country safely. This was a high priority so it was very important to have someone watching out for the enemy. It was very important to have someone standing guard.

Standing guard meant you might have to lose some sleep. Standing guard meant you might have to sacrifice a meal or two. Standing guard meant you might have to put yourself in danger for the good of the person or persons you are protecting. Standing guard could mean you might lose your very own life.

Here's the question I have for you is, "Who is standing guard over your marriage? Who is protecting your interests and your most precious possessions? Who cares enough to see to it that your marriage survives and is successful? Who or what is the enemy to your marriage? Who is standing guard? "

As I continued to watch these episodes week after week, I noticed one thing they all had in common. They all encountered enemies. Now the men were primarily responsible for keeping the people on the wagon trail safe. Although women did their part to help assure safety as well. Some of the enemies they encountered were wolves, coyotes, snakes and other creatures. Sometimes the enemy was within their campsite. Native Americans, although they were called Indians, on the show were perhaps their number one enemy.

Week after week, I watched these TV people programs face problems and their enemies. However, the people in these programs were actresses and actors. They each auditioned for their parts even the part of playing the enemy. Marriage is not an act and the enemies to marriages are a reality.

Here are a few enemies to marriages:

Not spending quality time together.
Not being truthful with each other.
Not being faithful or committed to the relationship.

However, what isn't an enemy to marriage is love. When love is standing guard over one's marriage the enemy has to relinquish its power.

And marriage's greatest love is...defense.

Now, that's protection.

Are You a Planner or Are You Spontaneous?

Many high school students make plans to go to college or move from their parent's home long before graduation day. Before a person moves from one country to another, one state to another, one city to another or just across town they usually have a plan of action on how to get there. Before a baker makes a cake or seamstress makes a garment they plan for the details. Before a contractor builds a home or a car manufacture builds a car they formulate a plan for accomplishing their goal. How you guard you marriage is a plan of action no one else can put in place?

My husband called from work early one Thursday afternoon and said he was having an extremely rough day. He said he just wanted to rest when he got home. He said he knew we had some unfinished chores to do, but he would like to do them another day.

It seems wives can always find something for their husbands to do. Paint this! Trim this! Cut this! Move this! Empty this! Carry this! Push this! Throw this away! Put this here! And the most important one of all, can you stop by the store and pick up some, get some...? Guess what? I am one of those wives as well. I know when I ask my husband to do certain things, it's not that I can't do some of them for myself, I just want him to know that he's still needed.

But after I got his call, I had no intention of putting him to work. Yet, I had to make him think I really wanted him to get the chores done before the weekend. So I sat out to make a plan. When he got home I asked him to get into my car. I told him I needed him to go somewhere with me, that I needed to pick up something and it might require his help. He gave me a look and so I said please. Please with my sugar on top.

He said, he really didn't want to and could it wait until Saturday. "Not really," I replied as I gave him the look (the wife look). He retorted "Okay, but I don't want to have to get out of the car," and without any hesitation he added, "Peggy, I don't want to argue about it." "I don't want to argue about it either,

I can promise you that", I responded. Smiling at him I commented, "It'll be to your advantage." He came back with, "Well can we just go do whatever it is you want to do so we can hurry up and get back here. I need to shower and get some rest?" "Yes," I announced calmly.

What he wasn't aware of was that I was planning an afternoon with rest in mind. What he didn't know was that I had packed the trunk of the car with a blanket and two pillows. "So where are going," he asked, upon getting into my car? "You'll see," I answered. "Peggy is this going to take a long time," he asked? Somewhat irritable he asked, "Peggy, what are you up to?" I told him just relax. He blurted out, "I could do just that if I were home." "I know," I said, but just give me a few more minutes."

Our first stop was at the gas station where I picked up some sodas. Our next stop was at Pizza Hut to pick up a large supreme pizza which had been called in just before we left home. He began to relax a little after we picked up the pizza. He was even pleasantly surprised when we started to reach our final destination which was Jacobson Park. Approaching the entrance he expressed how nice it was going to be to be away from the phone ringing and knocks at the door. He was glad not to have to think about work (as in house chores) or his day job at least not until the next morning.

We drove throughout the park until we found a place to stop to eat our pizza and drink our sodas. We found a place in the back of the park, a secluded spot with no children running around. A quite place away from everything well almost everything.

We sat and talked. We laughed. We told each other jokes. We ate pizza and drank sodas. We didn't have much money, so we had to come up with inexpensive ways to go on dates. We encouraged each other. We hugged. We kissed. We laid on the blank and looked up at the sky. We noted what the clouds looked like to each other. We ate more pizza and drank more sodas. We enjoyed the quiet. We enjoyed each other's company.

Around eight o'clock people started leaving the park. The park however, didn't close until dark, so we decided to stay longer. Then it happened, there was a smell, a disgusting smell. A nauseating smell. And suddenly we had visitors. Unexpected visitors! A family of five. Two adults and three black and white long busy tail creatures. SKUNKS!

Of course we packed our things without using any organizational skills and high tailed it out of there with no hesitation on his part to help pack up our belongings. It was a delightful date as well as a simple low cost date. We were glad we had finished eating before the uninvited guest showed up. Can you imagine how the date would have turned out if we had been sprayed?

Many couples make plans for date nights and that's not unusual with the way people's schedules are. We pencil them in on calendars and we save the date in our phones. Yet, all dates don't need planning out. Sometimes a spontaneous date is all that is needed.

So let me ask you a question when was the last time you and your spouse had a *spontaneous date*? Can't remember can you? When was the last time you just dropped everything and went on a date? When was the last time you just decided to go out and get your favorite dessert? When was the last time you just left the dirty dishes in the sink and the laundry undone and went to see a movie? When was the last time you decided at the spare of the moment to take your spouse window shopping? When was the last time you came home from work and said, "Honey, get in the car, I have some place I want to take you?" Remember everything doesn't have to be planned out and it doesn't have to cost a lot of money or any money for it to be a date.

So what about stopping what you are doing right this moment and go on a *spontaneous date*. After all *spontaneous dating* is just another way to safeguard your marriage.

Are You Going to Carry All That Luggage?

I love to go on vacations. When I can't go on long vacations I really enjoy taking little mini retreats. You probably love them too. And I dare say you already have a place or two in mind as you are reading this. A beachfront, afar away island or some exotic country. But with vacations and mini retreats there's packing to be done. Now packing can be very exciting because the thought of getting away is thrilling. However, at other times packing can be a chore. Work! It can especially become work if you are packing for more than one person.

You have to decide what to take and what not to take. You have to decide if you need a jacket, or a coat. You have to decide how many shoes you're going to need. If children are involved in your packing decision, you wonder if you have packed enough outfits for them. Sometimes you pack and then unpack. Then you have to pack and unpack until you get everything into the luggage you think you're going to need or at least you think you will need. Again I say, its work. The kind of work you don't get paid for unless it's part of your working career. Sometimes the luggage you pack is so heavy you can't pick it up. So you find yourself needing help to lift it.

Ok, I know you get the picture I am painting. But there's a reason I took so long to talk about packing one's luggage. When we get married we bring luggage from our past into our marriages. Some marital luggage could be unresolved conflicts from old family issues. Some martial luggage might include carrying results from a divorce - yours or your parents. Perhaps the luggage is carrying unbearable childhood memories or it could be that your luggage is so weighed down from your past relationships that you don't even want to face them or even talk about them. Sometimes you pack things you don't even need for the trip. And sometimes you have to borrow luggage to be able to carry everything you want to carry. Sometimes you leave something out of the luggage and have to go back inside the house or apartment to get it.

Each of the above scenarios have contributed some luggage brought to a marriage either yours or someone else you probably know.

Yet, the only way to deal with too much luggage even in a martial relationship is to deal with it like you are packing or unpacking luggage. You have to unpack the clothing or article one piece at a time. And so it is with the issues you may be experiencing in your marriage. You have to deal with them one at a time. One problem at a time.

Because, the truth is you will enjoy your marriage more if it's not loaded down with or weighed down with luggage from the past. Remember, sometimes the luggage isn't luggage from years gone by, sometimes it's the luggage you have from just a few days ago.

Let's pretend you are packing for your favorite vacation spot. You anticipate being there for several days. You are looking forward to it. Now, let's imagine that every piece of clothing or personal item you pack in your luggage represented the issues you were facing in your marriage. Let's pretend you were drinking a can of pop or soda (red of course) as other people call them, when suddenly it slipped from your hand and fell into the luggage. Now the soda is getting all over your favorite outfits. What do you do? Stand and watch it spill all over the rest of your clothing? No, you hurry to get your clothing or articles out of the luggage before any damage is done. You rush to get the clothes out of the luggage before they get wet or stained.

Luggage is for carrying things from one destination to another. Luggage is a container that holds personal valuables. But luggage isn't only for carrying things, it's also used to protect valuables from the outside environment.

I have several questions for you.

Are you taking every precaution to insure you aren't hoarding things from your past relationships in your marriage?

Are you taking every precaution you can to eliminate things that could be a hindrance to your marriage?

Are you making sure outside influences from other people aren't affecting your own marriage?

Are you doing everything you can to safe guard your marriage?

Come to think of it I need to give some thoughts to these same questions. So I've got to stop for now check on my meatloaf and take an inventory of myself. Then go pack. I need a vacation. No, I should say my husband and I need a vacation?

Got any suggestions?

Though Meatloaf and Marriage brought you smiles, laughter and, probably, puzzled expressions on your face, it challenges you and your marriage by asking questions throughout the book.

So it would be a mistake not to ask you yet another question at the end of the book. Here it goes.

Did you notice anything interesting about the words that answered the question, "What do meatloaf and marriage have in common?" For both meatloaf and marriage to be successful, you need the proper ingredients, seasonings and the right container.

Yes, it was a simple, yet profound book. But it shows you that marriage can be successful if you are willing to incorporate a team effort of love, commitment, communication, and safe guarding one another to help process, produce, and shape a successful marriage.

THE AUTHOR

Peggy B. Dixon has been successfully married to her husband, Walter (Pete) R. Dixon for over forty years. Her honest commitment as wife and mother is to be commended.

Peggy is an excellent teacher. She captures your attention by her impeccable demonstrations and reaches you with her insightful knowledge about marriage. She believes it is her responsibility to help make healthy marriages. Peggy does this by strengthening marriages through mentoring, coaching, counseling couples and holding workshops.

Peggy's forty plus years of marital experience allows her the opportunity to express her heart and provide you the ingredients you need to make your, "Meatloaf & Marriage" work.

For booking and more information contact peggybrucedixon@gmail.com

Meatloaf & Marriage

Are you in need of ingredients to help hold your marriage together?

Then Meatloaf & Marriage is a must read.

You want surprises?

Meatloaf & Marriage provides them.

Need sound advice?

Meatloaf and Marriage furnishes it.

If you want a return on your marriage,

Meatloaf & Marriage is a wonderful investment.

If you are looking for a book that provides hope for your marriage,

Meatloaf & Marriage provides you with over 40 years of marital experience.

And if you aspire to having a better marriage,

Meatloaf & Marriage is definitely the book to have in your possession.